FRANCHISING IN INDIA 2014

Legal and Business Considerations

KENDAL H. TYRE, JR., EXECUTIVE EDITOR
DIANA VILMENAY-HAMMOND, MANAGING EDITOR
PIERCE HAESUNG HAN, ASSISTANT EDITOR

LEXNOIR FOUNDATION

FOURTH QUARTER 2014

LexNoir Foundation is the charitable, educational arm of LexNoir, an international network of lawyers connecting the African Diaspora.

This publication, *Franchising in India 2014: Legal and Business Considerations*, contains excerpts from *Franchising in Asia 2014: Legal and Business Considerations*. Both works are published by LexNoir Foundation and reflect the points of view of the authors and editors as of the date of publication and do not necessarily represent the opinions, interpretations, or positions of the law firms or organizations with which they are affiliated, nor the opinions, interpretations or positions of LexNoir Foundation or LexNoir.

Nothing contained in this book is to be considered as the rendering of legal advice, either generally or in connection with any specific issues or case. Readers are responsible for obtaining advice from their own legal counsel or other professional. This book, any forms and agreements or other information herein are intended for educational and informational purposes only.

www.lexnoir.org

Table of Contents

Page

Franchising in India

Preeti Mehta
KANGA & CO.

Page

Bibliography of International Franchise Resources

Kendal H. Tyre, Jr., Diana Vilmenay-Hammond, Pierce Haesung Han & Keri McWilliams
NIXON PEABODY LLP

Acknowledgment

This book could not have been written without the hard work and dedication of each of the contributing authors and editors. Thank you.

We would like to acknowledge and extend our heartfelt gratitude to Maria Stallings of the Washington, D.C. office of Nixon Peabody LLP for her invaluable assistance in revising, proofing, and editing this publication.

About the Editors and Authors

Kendal H. Tyre, Jr. – Kendal is a partner in the Washington, D.C. office of Nixon Peabody LLP. He handles domestic and cross-border transactions, including mergers and acquisitions, joint ventures, strategic alliances, licensing, and franchise matters.

In his franchise and licensing practice, Kendal counsels domestic and international franchisors, franchisees, licensors, licensees and distributors regarding U.S. state and federal franchise laws as well as foreign franchise legislation in a variety of jurisdictions. Kendal drafts and provides advice with regard to franchise and license agreements, disclosure documents and area development agreements and has extensive experience drafting and negotiating a variety of other commercial agreements. His client base spans the United States and foreign countries, including South Africa, Kenya, and the United Kingdom.

Kendal is a frequent contributor to franchise publications and a frequent speaker at franchise programs held by the American Bar Association's Forum on Franchising and the International Franchise Association.

Kendal is co-chair of the firm's Diversity Action Committee and its Africa Group. Kendal is also the executive director of LexNoir Foundation.

E-mail address: ktyre@nixonpeabody.com

Diana Vilmenay-Hammond – Diana is an attorney in the Washington, D.C. office of Nixon Peabody LLP. She is a member of the firm's Franchise & Distribution Team.

In her franchise practice, Diana works with domestic and international franchisors on transactional and litigation matters. Specifically, she counsels franchisor clients regarding state and federal franchise laws, disclosure and registration obligations. Diana drafts and negotiates various commercial agreements, including international franchise and development agreements.

Diana has co-authored numerous articles on franchising and frequently co-hosted the Nixon Peabody franchise law webinar series. Topics have included:

- "Franchise Case Law Round-Up: Implications for Your Franchise," February 15, 2012;
- "Social Media Part II: Best Practices in Protecting Your Brand in the New Media," September 14, 2010; and
- "The Awuah Case: Bellwether or Outlier," May 11, 2010

Diana received her J.D. from Howard University School of Law and her B.A. from Georgetown University. She is a member of the American Bar Association (Forum on Franchising).

Email address: dvilmenay@nixonpeabody.com

Pierce Haesung Han – Pierce Haesung Han is an associate in Nixon Peabody's Global Business & Transactions Group, where he works with clients on three main areas.

- Mergers & Acquisitions: Providing assistance to both public and private clients with various mergers and acquisitions, performing due diligence, drafting and negotiating transaction documents, and facilitating closing and post-closing mechanics.

- International Commercial Transactions: Drafting and negotiating a variety of commercial agreements, including international franchise and development agreements, license agreements, and purchase and sale agreements.

- Federal Securities Law Matters: Assisting public and private clients regarding federal securities laws and stock exchange rules relating to corporate governance and disclosure.

Pierce received his J.D. from Georgetown University Law Center and his B.A. from Case Western Reserve University. He is admitted to practice in the State of New York and the District of Columbia.

E-mail address: phan@nixonpeabody.com

Keri McWilliams – Keri is an associate in the Franchise & Distribution team of Nixon Peabody LLP. Keri works with clients on a number of franchising issues, including obtaining and maintaining franchise registrations in various states, responding to state inquiries regarding trade practices, ongoing compliance with state and federal regulations, and updating franchise disclosure documents. She also handles franchise sales counseling and franchise system issues.

Keri is also an experienced general commercial litigator, who has handled a wide range of cases including copyright, trademark, and other intellectual property disputes, breach of contract cases, non-competition disputes, collection cases, and shareholder disputes.

Keri is a member of the American Bar Association's Forum on Franchising, and the Federal and Minnesota State bar associations. She is also a member of Minnesota Women Lawyers and the Minnesota Association of Black Lawyers, and a volunteer in the Volunteer Lawyers Network.

Keri received her J.D. from the Georgetown University Law Center and her B.F.A. from Washington University. She is admitted to practice in the District of Columbia and Minnesota.

E-mail address: kmcwilliams@nixonpeabody.com

Preeti Mehta – Preeti is a Partner of Kanga & Co. Preeti's practice is focused on foreign investment and joint ventures, mergers and acquisitions, private equity investment, corporate law, capital markets, franchising, and banking law. She has been recognized as one of the Leading Lawyers by the International Who's Who of Merger & Acquisition Lawyers and by Chambers & Partners for Corporate and M&A.

Preeti is also internationally recognized for her franchise expertise and has been recognized as one of the Leading Lawyers by the International Who's Who of Franchise Lawyers for the last several years. She chairs the legal committee of the Executive Council of the Franchise Association of India. Additionally, she serves on the Editorial Advisory Board of the International Journal of Franchising Law and has contributed to the India chapter of the International Encyclopedia of Franchising.

Preeti received her B.A. and LLB from Bombay University in 1981 and 1984, respectively. She also completed specialized franchise coursework at the Middlesex University, U.K. in 2000. Preeti first became an Advocate of the High Court, Bombay and Member of the Bar Council of Maharashtra in 1984 before becoming a Solicitor in Bombay and England in 1987.

E-mail address: preeti.mehta@kangacompany.com

About the Book

Franchising in India 2014: Legal and Business Considerations contains excerpts from the larger work *Franchising in Asia 2014: Legal and Business Considerations*. Both books serve as practical, succinct, easy-to-use reference tools for lawyers, business people and academics to use in navigating the laws and business issues impacting franchise arrangements in Asia.

This book provides an overview of the franchise industry in India and addresses the typical legal issues confronted when expanding a franchise system in India. The larger work, *Franchising in Asia 2014: Legal and Business Considerations*, covers those laws governing franchising in several other Asian countries.

In both books, an author, who is a legal expert in the designated jurisdiction, addresses the basic questions that a franchise lawyer would need to know to competently represent a client in expanding their franchise system to that country.

Each country chapter organizes a discussion of that country's laws under various headings and in a uniform format. Topics were sent to each country's author in the form of a questionnaire, and each author drafted responses to the questions presented. A general overview relating to the political and economic history of the country at the beginning of each chapter provides an initial context for the regulatory framework.[1]

Apart from an overview of the legal framework for franchising, each book contains other articles and resources that should prove useful to those in the franchise industry.

---

1 The source of information for these sections is the Central Intelligence Agency, https://www.cia.gov/library/publications/the-world-factbook/ (last visited October 25, 2014).

The authors for each chapter are listed at the beginning of a chapter and their biographical information is listed in the previous section, *About the Editors and Authors*.

Readers should always consult with local counsel in the relevant jurisdiction instead of relying solely on the information contained in this book. The laws governing franchising are evolving and local counsel in India are best positioned to provide timely, relevant advice applying the current law to the particular facts of a case.

Franchising in India

Preeti Mehta
KANGA & CO.
Mumbai, India

India

I. Introduction

A. Historical Background of Country

By the 19th century, Great Britain had become the dominant political power on the subcontinent. The British Indian Army played a vital role in both World Wars. Nonviolent resistance to British rule, led by Mohandas Gandhi and Jawaharlal Nehru, eventually brought about independence from Britain in 1947.

Communal violence led to the subcontinent's bloody partition, which resulted in the creation of two separate states, India and Pakistan. The two countries have fought three wars since independence, the last of which in 1971 resulted in East Pakistan becoming the separate nation of Bangladesh. India's nuclear weapons tests in 1998 caused Pakistan to conduct its own tests that same year. In November 2008, terrorists originating from Pakistan conducted a series of coordinated attacks in Mumbai, India's financial capital.

In January 2011, India assumed a nonpermanent seat in the UN Security Council for the 2011-12 term.

Despite pressing problems such as significant overpopulation, environmental degradation and extensive poverty, rapid economic development is fueling India's rise on the world stage.

B. Economy of Country

India is developing into an open-market economy, yet traces of its past policies remain. Economic liberalization, including industrial deregulation, privatization of state-owned enterprises, and reduced controls on foreign trade and investment, began in the early 1990s and has served to accelerate the country's growth, which has averaged more than 7% per year since 1997.

India's diverse economy encompasses traditional village farming, modern agriculture, handicrafts, a wide range of modern industries, and a multitude of services. Slightly more than half of the work force is in agriculture, but services are the major source of economic growth, accounting for nearly two-thirds of India's output, with less than one-third of its labor force. India has capitalized on its large educated English-speaking population to become a major exporter of information technology services and software workers.

In 2010, the Indian economy rebounded robustly from the global financial crisis - in large part because of strong domestic demand - and growth exceeded 8% year-on-year in real terms. However, India's economic growth began slowing in 2011 because of a tight monetary policy, intended to address persistent inflation, and a decline in investment, caused by investor pessimism about domestic economic reforms and about the global situation. High international crude prices have exacerbated the government's fuel subsidy expenditures, contributing to a higher fiscal deficit and a worsening current account deficit.

In late 2012, the Indian Government announced reforms and deficit reduction measures to reverse India's slowdown. The outlook on India's medium-term growth is positive due to a young population and corresponding low dependency ratio, healthy savings and investment rates, and increasing integration into the global economy.

India has many long-term challenges that it has not yet fully addressed, including poverty, inadequate physical and social infrastructure, limited non-agricultural employment opportunities, inadequate availability of quality basic and higher education, and accommodating rural-to-urban migration.

C. Franchise Legal Overview

Franchising in India is at an early stage and there is no franchise specific legislation that regulates the licence or sale of franchise rights. It is governed by a number of statutes, rules and regulations e.g. *The Indian Contract Act, 1872, the Trademark Act, 1999 etc.*

II. Regulatory Requirements

A. Pre-sale Disclosure

Please describe any pre-sale franchise disclosure or similar requirements that may apply to franchise transactions.

Laws of India do not require any pre-sale franchise disclosure or other requirements in respect of franchise transactions.

B. Government Approvals, Registrations, Filing Requirements

Please describe any necessary government approvals, registrations, or filing requirements that may apply to franchise transactions.

There is no approval, registration or filing requirement for entering into or carrying out franchise transactions under Indian law other than the reporting and registration requirements (*See* Section II (Currency)) as mentioned below. A domestic franchisee is permitted to make payments to a foreign franchisor without obtaining any approval from the government or the Reserve Bank of India. However, such payments are required to be made through an authorized dealer (i.e., a bank). See Section II for the requirements of submitting an application-cum-declaration with an authorized dealer for the purpose of remittance and see also Section IV of this chapter for information about the registrations required for trademarks.

Personal and corporate guarantees by a resident in favor of a non-resident are permitted without the approval of the Reserve Bank in very limited situations which would normally not cover franchise or other commercial transactions. Accordingly, the issue of corporate or personal guarantees by a resident in favor of a non-resident franchisor would require prior approval of the Reserve Bank of India. The Reserve Bank of India can take two to three months to approve such guarantees.

C. Limits on Fees and Typical Term of Franchise Agreement

Please describe any limits upon the nature and extent of fees and the term of a typical franchise agreement.

Indian law does not set any limits or caps on the types or amounts of fees and the tenure of a franchise agreement. In this regard, the parties may contractually agree upon the desired terms and conditions in the franchise agreement.

III. Currency

If all payments under a franchise agreement must be made in immediately available U.S. Dollars, please advise as to any restrictions, reporting requirements, or regulations concerning the exchange, repatriation or remittance of U.S. Dollars.

The purchase of, or the payment for use of, a trademark or franchise, is a current account transaction under the Foreign *Exchange Management (Current Account Transaction) Rules, 2000* and does not require any prior approval from the government or the Reserve Bank of India.[2] Payment can be made in freely convertible currency including U.S. Dollars, Euros and British Pound Sterling. There are no further restrictions with respect to which currency can be used to make payments; provided payments are made using any freely convertible currency. However, any payment by a resident to a non-resident would be required to be made through an authorized dealer.

In this regard, standard procedures are prescribed for the resident franchisee to follow whereby, the franchisee is required to designate a branch of an authorized dealer through which it would make remittances to the non-resident franchisor. The franchisee is also required to furnish an application-cum-

[2] The Reserve Bank of India was established in 1935 pursuant to the *Reserve Bank of India Act, 1934*. The bank is India's central banking institution and its responsibilities include formulating monetary policy among other duties.

declaration to the authorized dealer in the specified format providing the purpose of the payment.

IV. Taxes, Tariffs, and Duties

Please do not provide any in-depth comments on tax structuring. However, please provide your general comments on the typical amount of withholding tax that would apply and whether a "gross-up" provision contained in a franchise agreement would be enforceable in your country.

The income generated by the franchisor and franchisee in India would be subject to tax under the *Income Tax Act, 1961*. A franchisee is required to withhold tax on the payments to be made to the franchisor. The applicable rate of withholding tax for payment towards royalties and technical services is the lesser of (i) 10% and (ii) the rate prescribed in the double tax avoidance agreement between India and the relevant country to which remittance has to be made.

Further, a gross up provision contained in a franchise agreement is enforceable in India.

India has entered into double tax avoidance agreements with a number of countries,[3] including the United States, which provides relief from the double taxation of income derived from cross border transactions on which tax has been paid in India under the *Income Tax Act, 1961* and the income tax laws of the other country involved, respectively.

[3] India has double taxation avoidance treaties with: Armenia, Austria, Australia, Bangladesh, Belarus, Belgium, Botswana, Brazil, Bulgaria, Canada, China, Cyprus, Czech Republic, Denmark, Finland, France, Germany, Greece, Hungary, Iceland, Indonesia, Ireland, Israel, Italy, Japan, Jordan, Kenya, Korea, Kuwait, Kyrgyz Republic, Libya, Malaysia, Malta, Magnolia, Mauritius, Montenegro, Morocco, Namibia, Netherlands, Nepal, New Zealand, Norway, Oman, Philippines, Poland, Portuguese Republic, Qatar, Romania, Russia, Saudi Arabia, Serbia, Singapore, Slovenia, South Africa, Spain, Sri Lanka, Sudan, Sweden, Switzerland, Syria, Tanzania, Thailand, Trinidad and Tobago, Turkey, Turkmenistan, Uganda, Ukraine, United Arab Emirates, United Kingdom, United States, Uzbekistan, Vietnam and Zambia.

V. Trademarks

Please advise us as to whether there are any special requirements for granting a valid trademark license, including the use of a registered user agreement or a short trademark license agreement and any required filing of such an agreement with the trademark authorities.

In India, trademarks are governed by the *Trade Marks Act, 1999*. A registered trademark is one which is registered in the Register of Trade Marks under the *Trade Marks Act, 1999*. In the case of the infringement of a registered trademark, the owner of such trademark can take an action of infringement available under the statute. Whereas, in the case of infringement of an unregistered trademark, remedy is only available under the common law tort of "passing-off."

Trade Marks Act, 1999 does not provide for the licensing of trademarks. However, it deals with the appointment of a "registered user". A registered user does not have any right of assignment or transfer, but can institute infringement proceedings. To appoint a person as the registered user of trademark, a joint application by the owner of the trademark and the proposed registered user is required to be filed with the Registrar of Trade Marks. So long as an application is filed properly, it cannot be rejected by the Registrar of Trade Marks. However, there is no time specified for grant of approval by the Registrar of Trade Marks. It is important to note that a person cannot be made registered user of a trademark which is not registered under the *Trade Marks Act, 1999*.

Parties can contractually agree about the licensing of an unregistered trademark and there is no requirement to file or report under the law. However, under such licensing, the rights of the licensor and the licensee shall be only contractual and not under the *Trade Marks Act, 1999*.

VI. Restrictions on Transfer

Please advise as to whether there are any restrictions (1) on a franchisor to restrict transfers by a master franchisee, any interest in a master franchisee, or the assets of the master franchisee or (2) the ability of a master franchisee to control and/or restrict transfers of a subfranchisee's rights under a master franchise agreement, interest in the subfranchisee, or the assets of the subfranchisee.

There are no restrictions under Indian law (a) on a franchisor's ability to restrict transfer by a master franchisee of any interest in the master franchisee or the assets of the master franchisee, or (b) on the ability of a master franchisee to control and/or restrict transfer of a sub-franchisee's rights under (i) a master franchise agreement, (ii) an interest in the sub-franchisee or (iii) the assets of the sub-franchisee. Hence, parties can contractually agree to such restrictions and the same would be enforceable by Indian Courts.

VII. Termination

Please advise us as to any laws relating to termination in your country, such as agency laws, required indemnity provisions, notice or "good cause" requirements, or other laws affecting termination of a franchise agreement. Please describe.

There are no specific laws that govern the termination of a franchise agreement and such action is governed by the contract between the parties.

VIII. Governing Law, Jurisdiction, and Dispute Resolution

A. Choice of Law of Foreign Jurisdiction

Please confirm whether the choice of law of a foreign jurisdiction would likely to be upheld under the law of the country, except for certain matters such as trademarks, bankruptcy and competition matters, which we assume would be governed by the law in your country.

The choice of law of a foreign jurisdiction under a franchise agreement between a resident franchisee and a non-resident franchisor is permitted under Indian law. However, in matters such as bankruptcy and liquidation, the governing law would be the law of the land of the party undergoing bankruptcy proceedings or liquidation. The Indian courts recognize and enforce the judgment/decree of the courts of another country which the Government of India has notified to be a reciprocating territory under Section 44A of the *Civil Procedure Code, 1908*. However, if the decree has been passed by a court of a country which is not notified under Section 44A of the *Civil Procedure Code, 1908*, then such a decree cannot be enforced by the Courts in India and in such a situation, the party seeking relief will have to file a suit before the Court in India to obtain the appropriate relief.

B. International Arbitration Dispute Resolution

Please confirm that a court in your country would honor an election of international arbitration dispute resolution, and therefore refuse to hear any disputes arising under a franchise agreement.

Arbitration and Conciliation Act, 1996 (of India) recognizes arbitration by a foreign/international dispute resolution body. India is also a signatory to the *Convention on the Recognition and Enforcement of Foreign Arbitral Awards* (the "New York Convention") and an arbitration award passed in a foreign arbitration is enforceable in India. However, in light of a recent judgment of the Supreme Court of India in the case of *Bharat Aluminium Company and Ors. vs. Kaiser Aluminium Technical Service, Inc. and Ors.*,[4] where parties have agreed to international arbitration at a venue outside India, then Part 1 of *Arbitration and Conciliation Act, 1996* (which among other

4 Reported as: *(2012) 9 SCC 552.*

things, provides for recourse to Indian courts for injunctive relief) shall not be applicable. Hence, if in an international arbitration, an injunctive relief is required to be obtained from a Court in India, then the venue for the arbitration should be in India.

IX. Non-Competition Provisions

If the franchise agreement prohibits the franchisee from engaging in certain competitive activities during the term of the agreement, and for a 12-month period after the termination or expiration of the agreement, please comment on the enforceability of non-competition covenants in your country.

Non-competition provisions are governed by Section 27 of the *Indian Contract Act, 1872* which states that an agreement in restraint of trade is void. The scope and application of Section 27 has been explained by judicial pronouncements of Indian Courts which decide the legitimacy of such negative covenants on the principle of reasonableness. Under this emerging principle, the contractual provisions of non-competition would normally be upheld by the Courts in India beyond the expiration of the term of the agreement provided such restrictions are reasonable in scope and are found to be necessary to protect the bona fide interest of the aggrieved party. Imposition of a non-competition restriction under a franchise agreement that prohibits a master franchisee from engaging in competitive activities during the term of that such franchise agreement and for a period of twelve months after the expiration of the agreement would be upheld by the Courts in India.

X. Language Requirements

Does the law in your country require that a franchise agreement be translated into the local language in order to be enforceable between the parties?

There is no mandatory requirement under Indian law with regards to any particular language therefore, English language may be used without the need for translation into a local language.

XI. Other Significant Matters

Please advise as to whether there are any significant matters not addressed above of which a franchisor should be aware in connection with its entering into a franchise agreement in your country.

The issues discussed above constitute the significant issues relating to franchising in India.

The Franchising Association of India is a leading franchise association whose principal contact is Mr. C.Y. Pal.

Barista, Costa Coffee, McDonalds, Mothercare, Next, Papa John, Pizza Hut, Subway, Wetzel Pretzel etc. are some of the international franchise brands that operate in India. Some of the Indian brands are Aptech, Café Coffee Day, Jawed Habib, Mainland China, Lakme, etc.

India

Bibliography of International Franchise Resources

Kendal H. Tyre, Jr., Diana Vilmenay-Hammond, Pierce Haesung Han & Keri McWilliams
NIXON PEABODY LLP
Washington, D.C.

I. General

Mark Abell, Gary R. Duvall, and Andrea Oricchio Kirsh, *International Franchise Legislation* B1, ABA FORUM ON FRANCHISING (1996)

Kathleen C. Anderson and Anthony M. Stiegler, *Put Muscle in Your Marks: Enforcing Intellectual Property Rights* W14, ABA FORUM ON FRANCHISING (1995)

Richard M. Asbill and Jane W. LaFranchi, *International Franchise Sales Laws—A Survey* W7, ABA FORUM ON FRANCHISING (2005)

Jeffery A. Brimer, Alison C. McElroy, and John Pratt, *Going International: What Additional Restraints Will You Face?* W4, ABA FORUM ON FRANCHISING (2011)

Michael G. Brennan, Alexander Konigsberg, and Philip F. Zeidman, *Globetrotting: A Workshop on International Franchising* 10/W8, ABA FORUM ON FRANCHISING (1994)

Michael G. Brennan, Alexander Konigsberg, and Philip F. Zeidman, *Globetrotting: Strategies for Launching U.S. Franchisors Abroad* 2/P2, ABA FORUM ON FRANCHISING (1994)

Christopher P. Bussert and Jennifer Dolman, *Regaining Your Trademark After Abandonment or Misappropriation* W7, ABA FORUM ON FRANCHISING (2011)

Ronald T. Coleman and Linda K. Stevens, *Trade Secrets and Confidential Information: Rights and Remedies* W2, ABA FORUM ON FRANCHISING (2000)

Finola Cunningham, *Commerce Department Helps Franchisors Go Global*, in FRANCHISING WORLD 63 (Dec. 2005)

Michael R. Daigle and Alex S. Konigsberg, *Meeting Off-Shore Disclosure and Contract Requirements* F/W13, ABA FORUM ON FRANCHISING (1992)

Jennifer Dolman, Robert A. Lauer, and Lawrence M. Weinberg, *Structuring International Master Franchise Relationships for Success and Responding When Things Go Awry* W22, ABA FORUM ON FRANCHISING (2007)

Gary R. Duvall, Paul Jones, and Jane LaFranchi, *Planning for the International Enforcement of Franchise Agreements* W6, ABA FORUM ON FRANCHISING (1999)

William Edwards, *International Expansion: Do Opportunities Outweigh Challenges?* in FRANCHISING WORLD (February 2008)

George J. Eydt and Stuart Hershman, *Bringing a Foreign Franchise System to the United States* W9, ABA FORUM ON FRANCHISING (2009)

William A. Finkelstein and Louis T. Pirkey, *International Trademarks* W15, ABA FORUM ON FRANCHISING (1991)

William A. Finkelstein, *Protecting Trademarks Internationally: Current Strategies and Developments* B3, ABA FORUM ON FRANCHISING (1996)

Stephen Giles, Lou H. Jones, and Lawrence Weinberg, *Negotiating and Documenting Complex International Franchise Agreements* W21, ABA FORUM ON FRANCHISING (2006)

Steven M. Goldman, Stephen Giles, Marc Israel, and Stanley Wong, *Competition Round Up from Around the World* LB2, ABA FORUM ON FRANCHISING (2004)

David C. Gryce and E. Lynn Perry, *Trademarks and Copyrights in the International Arena* 6/W4, ABA FORUM ON FRANCHISING (1993)

Kenneth S. Kaplan, Andrew P. Loewinger, and Penelope J. Ward, *System Standards in International Franchising* W14, ABA FORUM ON FRANCHISING (2005)

Edward Levitt and Jorge Mondragon, *A Survey of International Legal Traps and How to Avoid Them—Beyond the Franchise Laws* W20, ABA FORUM ON FRANCHISING (2007)

Ned Levitt, Kendal H. Tyre, and Penny Ward, *The Impossible Dream: Controlling Your International Franchise System* W4, ABA FORUM ON FRANCHISING (2010)

Michael K. Lindsey and Andrew P. Loewinger, *International (Non-U.S.) Franchise Disclosure Requirements* W9, ABA FORUM ON FRANCHISING (2002)

Andrew P. Loewinger and John Pratt, *Recent Changes and Trends in International Franchise Laws* W4, ABA FORUM ON FRANCHISING (2008)

Andrew P. Loewinger and Thomas M. Pitegoff, *Avoiding the Long Arm of the Law in International Franchising: Issues and Approaches* W8, ABA FORUM ON FRANCHISING (1995)

Craig J. Madson and Katherine C. Spelman, *Similarity and Confusion in the Intellectual Property Arena* W11, ABA FORUM ON FRANCHISING (1997)

Christopher A. Nowak, John Pratt, and Carl E. Zwisler, *Franchising Internationally with Countries with Opaque Legal Systems* W20, ABA FORUM ON FRANCHISING (2006)

E. Lynn Perry and John L. Sullivan Jr., *Trademark Compliance and Enforcement Techniques* E/W12, ABA FORUM ON FRANCHISING (1992)

Marcel Portmann, *Franchising Sector Proves Global Reach*, in FRANCHISING WORLD (January 2007)

John Pratt and Luiz Henrique O. do Amaral, *Civil Law for Common Law Practitioners (or How to Draft an Agreement for Use Overseas)* W4, ABA FORUM ON FRANCHISING (2002)

Kirk W. Reilly, Robert F. Salkowski and Geoffrey B. Shaw, *Determining the Rules of Engagement in Litigation Here and Abroad* W5, ABA FORUM ON FRANCHISING (2008)

Catherine Riesterer and Frank Zaid, *Basics of International Franchising* L/B2, ABA FORUM ON FRANCHISING (1997)

W. Andrew Scott and Christopher N. Wormald, *Stranger in a Strange Land: Contrasting Franchising in International Expansion* W2, ABA FORUM ON FRANCHISING (2003)

Donald Smith and Erik Wulff, *International Franchising: The Unraveling of an International Franchise Relationship* 15/W13, ABA FORUM ON FRANCHISING (1993)

Kendal H. Tyre and Phil Wilkins, *Who is Making an Impact on Diversifying Their Brands*, in FRANCHISING WORLD (June 2008)

Frank Zaid, Pamela Mills, and Michael Santa Maria, *Essential Issues in International Franchising* LB/1, ABA FORUM ON FRANCHISING (2001)

II. Asia

Stephen Giles, Andrew P. Loewinger, and Sherin Sakr, *Go East Young Franchisor: Franchising in Asia-Pacific Other Than China and India* W21, ABA FORUM ON FRANCHISING (2011)

Stephen Giles, *Franchising in Asia-Pacific Region, Who's Who Legal*: FRANCHISE 2012 (2012)

A. China

Ren Yanling, *Changes to Chinese Franchise Law: An improved Balance Between the Interests of Franchisors and Franchisees*, in INT'L JOURNAL OF FRANCHISING LAW 3 (2012)

China: New Franchsing Law, in INT'L JOURNAL OF FRANCHISING LAW 2 (2005)

Ella S.K. Cheong, *China*, in INTERNATIONAL FRANCHISING CHN/1 (Dennis Campbell gen. ed. 2011)

Yu Qin and Richard L. Wageman, *China*, in INTERNATIONAL FRANCHISE SALES LAWS China-1 (Andrew P. Loewinger and Michael K. Lindsey eds. 2010)

Mark Abell, Daniela C. Brito, and Paul D. Jones, *Franchising in the BRIC Markets (Brazil, Russia, India, and China)* W18, ABA FORUM ON FRANCHISING (2008)

B. Hong Kong

Andrea S.Y. Fong, *Hong Kong*, in INTERNATIONAL FRANCHISING HK/1 (Dennis Campbell gen. ed. 2011)

C. India

Preeti Mehta, *India—Termination of Master Franchise Agreements and the Consequences*, in INT'L JOURNAL OF FRANCHISING LAW 3 (2007)

Yoginder Pal, *Franchising in India*, FRANCHISING WORLD (October 2006)

Mark Abell, Daniela C. Brito and Paul D. Jones, *Franchising in the BRIC Markets (Brazil, Russia, India, and China)* W18, ABA FORUM ON FRANCHISING (2008)

D. Indonesia

Sigit Ardianto and Rivan F. Ramadhan, *Indonesia*, in INTERNATIONAL FRANCHISING INA/1 (Dennis Campbell gen. ed. 2011)

Rick Beckman and Ferry P. Madian, *Indonesia*, in INTERNATIONAL FRANCHISE SALES LAWS Indonesia-1 (Andrew P. Loewinger and Michael K. Lindsey eds. 2010)

Kendal H. Tyre, Jr. & Pierce Haesung Han, *The Ministry of Trade of Indonesia Limits Growth of Food and Beverage Franchises*, NIXON PEABODY LLP: FRANCHISE ALERT (February 2013)

E. Japan

Takenari Shimizu, *Japan*, in INTERNATIONAL FRANCHISING JAP/1 (Dennis Campbell gen. ed. 2011)

Souichirou Kozuka and Takashi Kanai, *Japan*, in INTERNATIONAL FRANCHISE SALES LAWS Japan-1 (Andrew P. Loewinger and Michael K. Lindsey eds. 2010)

F. Malaysia

Leela Baskaran, *Malaysia*, in INTERNATIONAL FRANCHISING MAY/1 (Dennis Campbell gen. ed. 2011)

Mohd Bustaman Hj Abdullah and Wong Sai Fong, *Malaysia*, in INTERNATIONAL FRANCHISE SALES LAWS Malaysia-1 (Andrew P. Loewinger and Michael K. Lindsey eds. 2010)

G. Singapore

Daniel Lim, Bernard Lui, Michele The, and Vanessa Chew, *Singapore*, in INTERNATIONAL FRANCHISING SIN/1 (Dennis Campbell gen. ed. 2011)

H. South Korea

Brendon Carr and Jae-Hoon Kim, *South Korea,* in INTERNATIONAL FRANCHISE SALES LAWS South Korea-1 (Andrew P. Loewinger and Michael K. Lindsey eds. 2010)

I. Taiwan

Wellington Liu and David Lu, *Taiwan,* in INTERNATIONAL FRANCHISE SALES LAWS Taiwan-1 (Andrew P. Loewinger and Michael K. Lindsey eds. 2010)

J. Thailand

Alan Adcock and Sriwan Puapondh, *Thailand,* in INTERNATIONAL FRANCHISING THA/1 (Dennis Campbell gen. ed. 2011)

K. Vietnam

Mai Minh Hang and Nguyen Anh Tran, *Vietnam,* in INTERNATIONAL FRANCHISE SALES LAWS Vietnam-1 (Andrew P. Loewinger and Michael K. Lindsey eds. 2010)

14639056.3

Printed in Dunstable, United Kingdom

91343674R00020